Ad

Put Your Boots on
and Dance in the Rain

"Madlyn Steinhart is a person with a mission. She is active in social causes, in building relationships, in observing nature, and in a deep love of words that lead to clarification and reconciliation. She urges readers to listen to their hearts and to confront situations eye-to-eye and face-to-face. She does not want to give in to noise and meaninglessness but urges compassion, seeing more closely and challenging herself and others to follow their passions. 'Have you nothing better to accomplish?' she asks. 'This is where you need to be.' She believes that all of us can do more to make small changes that have a big impact. The essence of her work is her love of words and the joy that poets feel as they write. "Poets make love to words," she says, and "writing is my forever friend/ always catching rainbows with me." Reading Maddy's poems, one realizes that nothing is static, that even when you are hurt the pain can be alleviated by reflection and time and that those who are deeply important to you will give you strength to cope with the vagaries of life."

~Renee Cherow-O'Leary, Ph.D., President Education for the 21st Century New York and Los Angeles

"Deeply personal, Maddy's poetry is her life philosophy both in its minutiae and its totality. Reinvention, righteousness, and recovery are recurring themes. Through her poetry, Maddy has found healing and optimism about life and love. Her passion for helping others to reimagine themselves comes through her connections to music, nature, and moments of humanity she sees in the world around her. She wants all of us to leave behind the pain of our past, wake up from the sometimes soul-crushing mediated world, and truly see the beauty around us and inside of us."

~Marieli Rowe and Karen Ambrosh
National Telemedia Council and The Journal of Media Literacy

Put Your Boots on and Dance in the Rain

A Book of Poems

Madlyn Epstein Steinhart

The Three Tomatoes Book Publishing

Published 2019
Printed in the United States of America
ISBN: 978-0-578-60530-2
Library of Congress Control Number: 2019918156

For information address:
The Three Tomatoes Book Publishing
6 Soundview Rd.
Glen Cove, NY 11542

Cover and interior images: iStock Photo

Cover design: Susan Herbst

Dedication

To Howie Steinhart, my best friend and love of my life.

More today, than yesterday.

"Those who never fit in are the ones that stand out."

~ Loni Venti ~

Contents

Agony and Turmoil

Recovery

Gratitude

Agony and Turmoil

Listening

Spent too much time just hearing
There in spirit but not heart
Scars never healed correctly
Can you be too blind to see what is obvious and right
under your nose
Accepting is the hardest thing to do
Unconditional love just doesn't apply here
Excuses need not apply
They have danced in your mind for way too long now
You were the broken toy they refused to play with or
engage
Being different was not part of their world
Narcissism just is what it is
Luckily, it chose not to embrace you
Are you listening

Give You a Reason to Cry

Mother Nature and her children still stops her in her
tracks
Makes you want to share it and give back
Movies move her to tears
Some lyrics start the flow
Stop crying or I'll give you a reason to cry
You never took the time to listen or want to know
why
How jaded and cold can one be
Narcissism is your goddess
Others don't really matter
Put yourself second best
Wasn't worried about the rest
Wanted to give up
Never a reason to try

Give you a reason to cry
Give you a reason to cry
Maybe that is why rainbow chaser seeks a deeper truth
Not a lie

Fact of The Matter

You can dislike someone you love
Sometimes it is so unclear
Then you hear the voice in your head
Reminding you
Others don't notice
Either they don't choose to do so
They see what they wish to see
Not what is truly there
It is clear when someone is so shallow
So narcissistic
You can no longer digest their environment
Someone can hurt you so badly
The person who should never hurt you at all
Truth is, it is what it is
They are who they are
They look at how a package is wrapped as opposed
To the contents and quality

When It Feels Wrong

It keeps you awake
It makes you feel awkward
You know what it is
Won't admit it
Refuse to deal with it
Causes appointments set and then postponed
Excuses turned into prescriptions for maladies of your
own design
When it feels wrong
Go inside yourself and trust your heart
Speak up or reach out so you can be heard
Somebody will listen and care

Sometimes Never Applies

When you have been thrown under the bus too often
When you are ignored like a once loved toy
When the words no longer have meaning
It is not the way you wanted it to be
Sometimes never applies and the door is hermetically
sealed because dealing with the pain makes
no sense anymore

Conditional

Listened more than possible
Realized sometimes you cannot repair broken things
Even when they are people that you love
You have to give up and walk on for your own good
The good of your life and how it is lived matters utmost
Going back for more feels like being forgotten
The toy ignored
The feelings squashed
It is not a contract
Not apologizing for being myself
Not apologizing for loving someone you should have
accepted long ago
Because I love him should have been enough
But it is never even for you because all your life has been
conditional
Farewell

✳ Never Will Be

Putting myself first
Just too sensitive and caring
Hoping the scars in my heart will heal
though the breaks have taken a toll
Forgiving what can't be fixed no matter how many times
I try
Can't go back there again
Never will be your scapegoat
Never will be what you expect of me
Never will underestimate what I am capable of
Never will be a day like this one again
Even though one should never say Never

Goes On

Go on
With your drama
With your conditional love
With whatever pleases you and makes you happy
Cause it is all about you always will be
Forgiving you isn't possible
Haven't got time for the pain or grief any longer
Won't go back there or go there again
As others give thanks today
My thanks is realizing that life goes on
And you will find it goes on without me

It Has Long Been Over

You are a disgrace
You disgust me
You are an embarrassment
You deserve to be alone
God will get you for this
The wounds are healed but the scars remain
Going back will lead nowhere
Moving ahead sets me free
Be happy
Be healthy
Have the greatest life
It has long been over
Sometimes you can't fix what is broken
Own up to it and realize the grief has ended
The punching bag is gone
Codependency found a new home

Under the Bus

That is where you threw me
Wonder how many others
Doesn't really matter
Been there done that
Truth is yesterday is where you live in my life
There you will dwell forever more
unlike the Raven
Amazing how much you don't remember
Selective or Deductive
Under the bus

No Band Aids

Stop the world
Time to get off
Too many values, hearts, and people broken
Too many stupid and pathetic surprises
Imbalances and no vacancy in what we have come to
know as society
We chose utopia and threw
beauty away
Some changes that are inevitable are not acceptable
Sweeping them under the rug and turning our backs
accomplishes nothing
Defining it as the new normal just lets us go with the flow
Optimism might point us towards a better direction
We need to heal
We need to talk
Face to face
Like we used to do
Not all of yesterday is bad
We have tuned out

We are members of too many clubs
There is one club that matters
The human race
There are no band aids to heal it
Common Sense
Dignity, Grace, and Respect
Accepting change by moving forward not backward

No Fixes

No more tears
Cried too many
Made myself so ill that blood pressure went sky high
You are not worth my health
There is no worth left
No words left to be said
Moving forward because to all of you
I am dead
No repairs
No apologies
Scars and wounds way too deep
No fixes just goodbyes

Memories

Colored photographs framed and some in scrapbooks
That is how I will remember you
You have chosen to forget what was meant
So long ago is today because that is all
that is left
No guilt, apologies, no second guessing
I will remember you
A year ago you forgot about me
Memories used to be great on rainy nasty days
Now, they are not cracked up to be
the way they used to be
Nor do they matter
You have selective memory
This is a broken heart that will never be
repaired by surgery
The scar is all that is left

If You Only Knew

Her heart was broken and shattered
After all this time just seeing you in the distance brought
it all back
Moved up
Moved on
Am loved and love
Leading someone on is beyond comprehension
But that was yesterday
Her todays are filled without the likes of you
If you only knew
Knowing now
Being flustered and tossed to the side because contour
matters more than size
It was about the size of a heart

Tears

Flowing slowly
Streaming angrily and rapidly
Reminding us of joy and pain
It's simply the way it goes
Sometimes it is necessary
Otherwise in expected ways
A cleansing of sorts but usually in a shower alone
Kleenex and towels befriend you
Until you are able to smile between the sobs

Ocean of Pain

If you swim in it, my apologies
If you drown in it, here is a life vest
The dirt and disgust can't be washed away
Feeling depressed never goes away although know
we are swans in waiting
The flashbacks are real
Please swim to the shore
Do what needs to be done so you can enjoy the ocean
with less pain and divine dignity

Not Above the Law

When you hurt somebody
When your acts break their soul
When loved ones stand by them or walk away
because there is nothing left for them to do
Are you listening in DC
Everywhere and all over the world
Be a loving and caring
Genuine human being
Get help if you need it
Admit your issues and face them
Those who don't qualify
You are not above the law
Your day will come to face the music
The Me Too movement is only the beginning
To right so many wrongs

Bullied

Used to be called teased
Try harassed
Try ignored
Don't try
You had to be there
You were different
Not like the rest
Going with the flow didn't occur to you
Now children have to deal with social media
It is anti-social
People die from being bullied
Society let go of chatting and talking face to face
No communication old school
Still not completely confident
I am me
For what it is worth
I was bullied
This maverick has no time for any of you

Footprints

Those hugs were supposed to last forever
Every rose you stopped to smell withered
Crystal hearts just don't beat loudly or not at all
The sea glass is smaller and the shells are all broken
Lovely echo gone
When did hearing replace listening
When did you give yourself back
You remain everything
that you used to be
Except that smile is painted on and stuck in time
Used to bes don't count anymore
Or do they Neil Diamond
You're talking but I don't need what you say
How many times can your tears bleed
We saw the footprints you left for us on the winds of the
sand

Mirage *

Lost horizon sky
No humans, cars, or bridges near an eye
No hocus pocus
No incantations
No dramatic situations
Your heartbreak is still so audible
You're so gone that getting you back is beyond
comprehension
Yet we reached you just before the fall took you home
Seems you have been lost in a desert of your own
creation for a very long time
It's all too real for you in your mirage

The Summer Wind

Dancing along Nova Scotia Bay
Every care and thought choreographed away
Remnants of a dream and glistening water on the sea
That yesterday and tomorrow were carefree
Running like a bull set free from a china closet looking
for a reason
Wanted a chance to change for now and every season
Remnants of a nightmare that continues repeating it's
the way things should be
He jumped and left us, he will never see
Wake up and feel the breeze on an autumnal day
Remember how the summer wind called to him when
he left us that day

Lessons

You talked of sacrifice
You rolled the dice
Substance was never ever important
Had you thrown the glitz and glamour away
Perhaps you would enjoy and savor each day
Not living your life through others
But for and through yourself
Reality not fantasy
You are who you are
Rainbows are technicolor not black and white
Will you ever learn the lesson

Forward

Not the lady in red
makes me uncomfortable
The cauldron in mind in bubbling overtime
How good are you supposed to be until you find out
what really matters
There are no angelic excuses here but the feeling is that
the answer is around
Around the corner looms
It's summer plus for me now and the seasons seem mixed
in a concoction unrecognizable
Reinvention and self-discovery feel like a backwards roller
coaster ride
Inside it feels like my world has to start so the ride
continues
forward throttle
Pushing the restart button

Recovery

Move On

Mistaken because you are so lost
You want to encounter found
It is not in a person or intangible object
It is in your heart and soul
If they are wounded no matter the scar
Give yourself the freedom and time to heal
Scars are reminders
Somethings can't be fixed
Neither can some people
It is never your job to do that
Even the broken rise again

Most of All

Long ago
Feels like yesterday
That is where you live in my heart
Hard to love a one way street
It was hormones overheating
Not interacting or shared
So when I go back there
That other time and place
Knowing what time has taught me
The second time around came to pass
When it was not
all encompassing
The hormones calmed down
Even now, he loves me most of all
As for you, hope you found your most of all
You are guilty of breaking a heart

Angels and Memories

They slip quietly into the night, pain free
my wish for all
Instead of social media and texting
Catching shows on marathon cable
Pick up the phone
Talk
Say what needs to be said
Listen very carefully
You don't want to think of people you love as memories
or angels
The toxic you let go of does not count here
You know who really counts
If you listen to your heart
Cherish those you have
Memories are made of moments and angels

Hold On

Utilize brain
Clamp the urge to open your mouth
Is it worth hurting somebody
It is golden
How about yourself
Have you nothing better to accomplish
Be a better citizen of the world
Strive to do your very best
Your thoughts
Your feelings
Sometimes better not shared
Hold on to them
The bittersweet might be more beneficial
So hold on tight

Finally

Dearest old friend
We are sharing our heart with others
My fears are still with me but the time is now
It is about emerging into the woman some really don't
know
The one who truly knows has my heart and keeps my soul
in check
Being sensitive is a double edged sword
Been there and done that
Second thoughts need to go the way of yesterday's news
It matters but it takes its place in herstory
Finally, we have something to say and it matters
As do others

Gull Serenade

They wake you in Hyannis with their Ha-Ha-Ha alarm
Gulls cry softly and then the chorus begins
Barely heard them on Martha's Vineyard
Remember them in Nantucket years ago
Yeow, Yeow, Yeow
Somehow echoing a sweeter crescendo
this time
In a time that needs solace, balance, respect, and unity
We welcome their song
Haoh, Haoh, Haoh
Long all
Humming and laughing on Main Street
Haoh, Haoh, Haoh

In Between Dreams

What really happens when you're in between
All the plans, wishes, and schemes
It's not always polka dots
and moonbeams
If it were, it wouldn't be worth it
But as you go, go your own way
Sleepless nights stop you dead in your tracks
Something similar to a mind attack
You take the time to re-evaluate
It is what it is or you go with the flow
Setting different things in motion
You have to be alone with yourself
Which is really not a bad thing
Listening to both your heart and your head
Equal time for both
Which is really not a bad thing when you're in between
dreams

Another Side

No ifs
No ands
No cant's
No buts
Get on with it
Have a conversation
Eye to eye
Face to face
Stop texting and social media cruising
Be appropriate
Or inappropriate
Don't let anybody decide for you
The remote control is no longer in your hand
Shouldn't have been in the first place
You have to have known the honesty
Understand the truth
Shake it off
Find a new direction
A new kind of strength
You want to know
Though you really might not want to

Doing the right thing isn't always popular
There is a wrong and right way
Once you've had enough
There is no going back
No need to return
No matter what you have tried
There's another side
That is where you need to be
Only you hold yourself back

Advice

What you hear and what you listen to
are worlds apart
What you take away is another story
You pick your fights
Self-editing becomes a talent you hone
Keep your friends close and enemies closer
Frenemies need not apply
Sometimes they are the same but you have to learn that
Then when you least expect it many things make
themselves clear
Just remember that every moment is a learning
opportunity
You should never ever stop learning
Advice to you is to remember that because when it does
You are no longer on this khaki coil
Keep your feet on the ground even when you are soaring

Shadow Walking

Locked in the horns of a dilemma
One conundrum folds into another
Like a cake with unfolded ingredients
Sometimes you feel separate and then apart
Life's curve balls requires adaptation, revision, rethinking
Yet, you take your seat at the table
Whatever you do criticism will follow
Going with the flow works for some
Shadow walking occurs in the wee hours of the morning
Wasn't it you I saw

Second Best

Sometimes third place
Always something better, brighter, prettier
Plain Jane became my moniker
Even when the one person who said it
Shouldn't have
She never knew better
Substance always took second place to appearance
Never got that message
So in the world of Hertz being the champ and Avis being
runner up
That is how it used to be
The mold was broken and second best is fine
Nobody to prove myself to but me

Who Said

Rules are made to be broken
Perhaps adapted
Truth needs to be spoken
Nothing is as easy as it looks
The trick is to make it look that way
When you listen don't read between the lines
The words will find you in good time
Who said
Who said
That you can't climb the mountain to your dreams

Synergy

Its origins are important to you
It is a balance of old school and new school thinking
The balance is the key
You are part of an army with help from people and places
you have known
Sometimes unknown if you have yet to encounter them
Take it in
Digest it
The drama will only bother you if you let it
Who said you have to do that
Get those echoing voices in your head out
Being different is not a life sentence
It is usually a gift you have to utilize
Embrace it and respect yourself
If you are happy than that is all that matters
Those you make unhappy will have to deal
Whether you know that or not
You are strong
You are powerful
You matter

Synergy is the game of life
Learn to play well
Kick chaos to the curb with its BFF drama
Never assume
For you know what that makes you
You are always a work in progress
Remember not to take nonsense from anyone

Been There

Down just doesn't work
Take a step back and then forward for up
You will get there
Not when you plan and then again when you are ready
You may or may not know that
Nobody will tell you
Learning continues when school has long been out
Let yourself in
Been there

What the Future Holds

Embrace and enjoy today
Yesterday is part of
your memories
Not every wrong has its remedy
Sometimes you just can't fathom things or people
Is it worth the effort
You can't always let go, give in, or forgive
Easier said than done
The choices are yours of course but by never saying never
What was and what might yet be
The door to your life remains ajar
for the success or failure of the future

Embrace and Release

Found you
Was searching but encountered the unexpected
Souls, stories, connections, family
Accepting every person and puzzle like the gems they are
What was and what is are in two different universes
Those that connect us are no longer here to tell their
stories
Knowing that finding things out might be surprising and
shocking
Still need to know why things happened and how we got
to now
Have to embrace and release

Lessons 2

Stuck in neutral situations
Knowledge and learning must accompany you
Walking through your fears
When will the freeing embrace you
Release yourself
So where do you go from here
Even if you don't know where you are going to
Standing still
Not regressing but on a trajectory of your own making
Perhaps not what you expected
Don't expect, accept
One step at a time
Baby steps if necessary
Finding whatever makes you happy and complete
When you arrive be prepared
The process is the most important asset
Change is the one constant
That can't be taken from you
Moving forward takes time
Lessons always being learned

Listen Carefully

Hearing is not required of you
Shut your mind off
Stop doing
Give your muse a break
Really concentrate
Enjoy mother nature's children
Take it all in
More than smelling the roses
Marvel at what others fail to notice
Listen carefully to the music and lyrics around you

Real

Don't mince words
Dislike phonies
Real and true
I am a poet
Taken long enough to say that aloud
Have no time for stupidity or unfair games
Very real
Time and effort precious

A Feral Cat Man

Bright blue bitter January sky
New York City Eskimos running their Sunday errands
Then he arrived with his seen better days car
Man with the mission
His cats were waiting
They scurried from nowhere to Bluebelt Park
Out of his bags came food for his cats
Watching and quietly seeing love and respect at a strange time in our cities
Love protected those homeless cats as my poetry protects me

Every Moment

The walking wounded
Don't exceed your respect
We walk on by with
our heads held high
probably because our shoulders are doing their best to
keep us together
Be thoughtful and kind
A smile and a hug go a very long way
Please remember that sometimes reaching out helps you
more than the person you gave your time to
How fragile we are
Appreciate every moment

Courageous Conversations

What needs to be said
Hard as that might be to listen to
Digest without commentary
Air gets cleared
Beliefs don't have to be agreed with
The direction you choose after airing the words
Is up to you
They are not easy to have
Sometimes your heart isn't up to it
Your head can't wrap itself around the circumstances
That is why they are courageous conversations
Sometimes it is easier to save your breath

The Best

The packages are being delivered
Well-wishers send greetings of joy and good cheer
Some people have loved ones near
Grow your backbone and constitution strong
Be good to yourself and find where you belong
The gift of your time and efforts happen every
day of the year
Do your utmost and your very best
It has nothing to do with all the rest
Stars only shine for those that take the higher road

Making Love to Words

This is not sex
Much higher level
Melding of spirit and soul
You don't lose control here
You polish and perfect it
Call to the muses for help
Listen for their call
Inspiration hugs you
Nothing to exchange
Sharing here leaves you spellbound
If you are lucky
Cherish what others don't take the time to find
You are a poet
You make love to words
The words teach you to love more than you thought
your heart could take

With My Head Up High

I have felt like nothing
I have felt like nobody
A forgotten plaything ignored while children
play with what's shiny and new
Picked last in teams at school
Once I made love to a piece of paper
Saw the beauty in phrases and words
Polished and rewrote until my pens bled
Like the Ugly Duckling
I became a swan because you love me
Learned to love myself
With my head held high

Getting Lost

Not in translation
In acceptance
The only constant is change
If you stay set in your ways
If you don't carry on when life gives you bumps
Open your heart and your mind
Keep learning life is a classroom
Not in schools or universities
Yesterday once more is a memory
Each day you get the opportunity to make a difference
The size of it does not matter just contribute to the world
Getting lost within yourself serves no purpose
You might get surprised
It is not about Baby Boomers, Generation x y z,
Millennials
Culture, tradition, and joy
Celebrate before it is too late
Getting lost serves no purpose because
you may never get found

Never Say *

You won't
You can't
Be ready and take a chance
Prepare to get your heart broken
The wounds will heal but the scars won't
Stand up tall with your head held high
Never say never
Believe it and be loyal to yourself
It is selfless not selfish
Never be a martyr

Fresh Air

You are wished a happy and healthy life filled with joy
and adventure
Keep those you love close to you
Be gracious and kind
It is not all and always about you
Whatever pleases you doesn't please others
So know that and move on
Family is defined many different ways
Sometimes relatives take their leave because they know
that they only belong under certain prescribed ways
It is not a membership
You don't have to renew
Breathing fresh air for the first time
Everybody is going through something
Choose what works best for you and pay others no mind
It is your time
Don't waste it

Goodbye ✿

Half of my life was spent with you
Thought there was so much more to do
Truth is that it isn't there
Perhaps it can't be seen
Maybe I no longer see it
Caring about you will always be there
Too many other soldiers in this army
Your essence is somewhat gone
Your star doesn't shine like it used to do
Perhaps it is time to say goodbye
Make room for the others
Time to go

Be Happy

Relish every moment
Enjoy what others don't take the time to notice
Smell the rose but remember the thorns
Remember that the flower is a four letter word
Embrace the outside of the box mindset
Enjoy the nectar of life
Be healthy
Be Happy
Stay as far away from me as you can

Broken

Sometimes you have to move on
You clean up the shards
Tread carefully
Cherish yesterday
Sometimes you can't fix what is broken
Life is short but even more so when
arguing and fighting is a priority
More important to live fully
When you are broken you learn to play differently
even if you do that alone but not lonely

Letting Go

No longer want to be a doormat
Co-dependency doesn't work for me
The way you live your life and see the world
Is a journey which leads me to nowhere or anywhere I
choose to be
May all of your dreams come true
May good health and happiness befriend you and yours
We have had yesterdays but no tomorrows
Been there
Done that
Letting go
My life is not a show on MeTV

Now

These are shallow times
Lacking depth and gratitude
Love that is pure and true
Scoffed at and dismissed
Dig deeper
Be stronger
Reach to places you have never known
Like asteroids trying to find a place in the galaxy
Many are so lost and just don't belong
Let's hope right now will find us brighter days
Lift someone up
Do the very best that you can everyday

Free

Your narcissistic life
Your pleasures
Feel free to be you and I will be me
Your way or the highway
You're thinking you know it all
Set my course on the best direction
You and your family were mourned
Guilt trips be gone
Can no longer go back to your drama
Much joy and happiness are wished to you and yours
We are happier and do much better
since we are free of you

But You Will

You will love again
It may not be the same and it might be better
Nobody has the right to tell you whom or how
Just be decent, kind, and genuine
You will laugh again
The tears will come and go at inopportune times
Dry your eyes and play your life forward
Friends and family will come and go
Wish them well
Be open if they return
The gems will always have your back
But you will
But you will

It Repeats Itself

Generations reunite because of music
Melody, harmony, lyrics
Yesterday once more enjoyed by younger people
Respect not only embraces souls but nothing really goes
away
Bring together the classics with new talent
It is not a reboot or a revival but something magical and
incredible
Long overdue
Listen with your heart
Don't let your head and social media get in your way
Tune in and it repeats itself

Shower Tears

Do you cry there too
The facts flow down the drain
They awaken you in flashbacks
Even with help and guidance
With lots of love and care
Once you make contact with the past
No matter how recent or long ago
Find your pain and find a path
Someday happiness will share those tears
You can only live happy if you welcome it

Words

life lesson posted
reimagined
rebooted
reconstructed
reworked
everything old is newer again
old school and new school merge to become one
beware the toxic
it's their chaos not yours
be determined to live and think outside of the box
rules are meant to be adapted not broken
be accepting, you don't have to agree
do things as robustly and happily as you can
stress destroys life and time to live it
as a late poetess friend told me long ago, do it to it

Trajectory

You can't lead if you can't fall or follow
Lessons continue to be learned daily
Get over yourself
Listening not hearing is essential
When you forgive don't forget
It's not easy and sometimes impossible
Let go because going backwards accomplishes nothing
As you rise and the door opens the trajectory is visible
Do your
best to embrace it and fight the fear
Choose to become what and who you are

No Matter

The mountains you climb from your chair
Even virtually
The achievements earned and gained
You will never
satisfy this person or people
So stop trying
Selfless means you are an enabler and a masochist
Despite and in spite of your efforts
You will never please a dissatisfied person
who should love you unconditionally
No matter

Excuses Be Gone

You threw it to the wind
Gusts of regret and unfinished business
You are good enough to live your life
Muddling through is never satisfying
The mannequin way of the going with the flow just
doesn't suit you
You are a maverick and that is just fine
You fell in love and learned to love yourself as well
It's your mind to change
Aren't you tired of standing still with shoe prints
all over you
Excuses be gone
Carry on

Freedom

Fear befriended me
A menace beyond belief
Held me for a ransom nobody should ever pay
Selfless means you are codependent and an enabler
Somehow life showed me somebody never recognized
before
When all else fails, marvel at the flight of butterflies
Freedom at last
This butterfly learned to use her wings
Watch her soar

Awesomeness

That word surrounds her
From the very moment we met
She will write and polish her words
Listen to the rhythm of the rain
Love her special somebodies
Especially one with a sunny effervescence
much like her own
She will watch the clouds dance
Enjoy the uniqueness of her spirit
Her awesomeness still remains and glows everlasting
Words have the power to break hearts
We will be mending but the healing begins
Her name is Loni Anne
But to me she is Awesome

Be Merry

Another year will soon be upon us
Make your heart and head friends
Contribute your time and effort where it suits you and
others
Your help, even in the smallest amounts of time is
appreciated
Do it your very own way
What others think really doesn't matter and never should
have
You awake everyday hopefully to do your utmost or at
least your very best
Don't live between a rock and a hard place
You choose your path and if it gets altered
you adjust and compromise
Be merry and deal

Survival

Getting by does not qualify it
Wish it had more quality
At least it looks that way
Perhaps that is the problem
Does one want to coast through their days
It might be easier but there lies the problem
Is that the very best you can do
Are we not supposed to strive for more
You know what used to bes and supposed to bes get you
Maybe that is why there are days when you want to stop
the world and get off of it
At least, it feels that way

Rainy Days ✗

Trick is to make it look easy
Take the higher plane and ground
Fake it 'til you make it
The butterflies will be in your gut
You will never be sure
Be your own true self
The naysayers won't stop talking
You will come through shining because nothing is easy
You are the only one to find happiness and gratitude
despite the rainy days
Put on your boots and dance

Gratitude

The Magic of You

Draw outside of the lines
Create a new color
Drink white wine with meat and red wine with fish
Sing off key, on key, any key at the top of your lungs
Wear unmatched clothing or last decade's style
Whatever way you define happy is fine with me
The cheer and support will be started by a source close to
your heart
I loved you then as I love you now
As I have from the start
How could anybody not love the magic of you

✱ Remember

Respect and gratefulness were precious
You knew who your friends were
You are open to enjoying others if you know your heart
You could enjoy every moment
Savor the magic because it was special
Cherish those around you near and far
Yesterday repeats itself again
You are no longer sure you can return to that time
Maybe the sweetness nugget means more than it ever did
before
Remember who you are
Remember what you believe and what you stand for
Remember to be involved in the life you were given
Life is an ongoing lesson
It does not only happen in school
You are here and that is the greatest gift of all

Special Someones

Platonic or not
In an instant, you know this is a life time one
The perfect recipe with the best ingredients
The It factor
The je ne sais quoi
You love them forever
The call late at night
The miss you too and meaning it
Time stands still even if it's been awhile because
It falls back into place so genuinely
It is a golden circle that envelopes you if you are lucky
enough to have it
Cherish those moments
Remember and embrace the good and bad times
Be grateful and true
Really listen
Special someones are hard to find but you will know
when you do
Lucky you

One More Time

It was gentle and quiet like a warm summer breeze
Gone too soon and passed you by
You can recall it and bring it back but it is never quite the
same
Maybe even better because it left an impression
That smile so unexpected
The kindness and generosity of a stranger
The toll paid for
The thank you
One more time
Precious and perfect in a world that needs so much more
and we can all make small changes toward it

✳ More Than Enough

You are good enough
You are sound enough
Unlike any other because you're original
Going through the laces and spaces
You listened and stopped hearing
Knowing that being different was a gift
Not something to be ashamed of or bullied about
You will take your place
Find your ten minutes of fame or more
Telling those who share your life what they have already
known
They may be seeing you for the very first time
Enjoy it

Unpolished Gem

It was there but she didn't know back then
Despite her cheerleaders the message didn't get through
Maybe she knew but didn't let on
Fortunately she emerged a swan and a gem of
luminescence and quality
Just being in her presence the obvious is clear
She forever shines if you get the honor to be in her life
A pleasure and a delight this gem
Long Island needs to know her
as do you

Writing

Befriended you long ago
Latch key kid doing what was expected
You let me talk to you
Life got in the way for others to have time for me
Never judged or bullied me
When life turned cruel
You glistened
Without you
Would have been gone long ago
You saved my life
Others have read you and shared their feelings too
Writing is my forever friend
Always catching rainbows with me

Henry David

Taught your books
Reread your words
Walked at Walden
Life changing moment
Touching your desk left me humbled
Always crafting words like reworking recipes
to improve them
Poets can't laugh at themselves, but their words
lessen life's highs and lows

Nothing But Memories

Better times
Easier days
Egos checked at the door
Days of what used to be
That is how you will be remembered
Today and Tomorrow passed us by
If you are happy that is what is best for you
That is all I can ask for
You are photographs and memories
That will have to be enough

Cherished

When you have reached the point of no return
despite the many times you've been burned
Somehow the pieces fall together and make sense
no more false starts, doubts, or pretense
no matter what happens and you think all has perished
Hold on, hang on, stand up tall with your head held high
because you are cherished
you remind me of that fact every moment of the year
you are loved, adored, and cherished
my dear

She Talks to Animals

Greets the squirrel chomping on his acorn
Knowing he sees her but scurries up his tree
Dogs jumping and hoping they get a pat on the head
Perhaps a scratch on the head
The very last butterflies of autumn
Now she stops to watch them and admire their finery
floating in the breeze
There is a respect and admiration as she enjoys what
others may not take the time out of their day to see
She talks to animals knowing how precious they are

Thankfulness

We have so much sadness and separation here and all
over the world
Some have it better than you do
Some a lot worse and the source is not the issue
Kindness and graciousness is not a lot to ask
A smile can be the kindest gesture
Listening can be a gift when somebody needs to vent
Take a moment to realize what you have
Remember those you lost as angels join the table no
matter where that might be
Try a little thankfulness

Any Stronger

My love for you has no beginning or end
It is pure and genuine
Still surprising and precious
After all these years filled with laughter and tears
It is
still you and always will be
Still lose control
Love you with a full heart and star gazing soul
There is no other

Friends

Poets don't have many
They are loners by heart and nature
Every now and then a surprise finds you
My poetry has always listened
Always been my friend
When you reach out
Read our words
Pass a genuine heart felt comment
Then you have the makings of a new friend

Blue Bird

Which of you were saying Hello
Smiling down
Sending a sign
Letting me know this too shall pass
We will get through this because tomorrow brings
another day
You are missed and remembered
Nice to know you are there

October Roses

Cream colored
Fuchsia blushed
All dancing on the wind
Spice rack colored leaves
paid them no attention
as the wind went unnoticed in the Big Apple

Falling

In love and love a treasure
He gave me his name and heart
When you don't look you find this magic
Be open and caring
It was not the first time I fell but
The second time around was the charm
My Prince Charming still surprises and delights me
No matter a Prince or Princess
Listen with your heart and head
Don't let others get in the way of your
falling
Your happiness should never be judged by the way of the
world
After all, it is your world

Inspiration

Hatched
Matched
Dispatched
Sometimes permanently excluded
for reasons beyond their control
Listen to their dreams
Encourage them to be brave
Regrets will happen
Part of the game
Trying is your best ally
Doors open when you least expect them to do so
Remember they slam shut as well
Take the word never out of your vocabulary
Your heart is absolutely worth it
You will find sooner or later that you are too
Shut off those voices in your head and
Tune into something unexpected

Say Yes

Watching squirrels perform acrobatics on phone wires
Admiring blue jays in October
Enjoying skaters at Rockefeller Center from a restaurant
window
Giving a donation to a homeless man and his canine
companion
Eating that Lindt chocolate very slowly
Taking a bubbly bath while drinking white wine in a
crystal goblet
Loving someone exactly like you did in a younger time
Say yes

Second Time Around

The first love
Puppy dog and exploding hormones
Hard to explain and harder to control
Then when you aren't looking
Prince Charming or Princess Charming appears
Just because you are you
Your grace and kindness
The look that another person didn't appreciate
Now matters
The second time around is forever
Just be ready to accept it when it comes your way

October Walk

Yes, she talks to creatures while admiring their acrobatics
on a phone line above
Monarch butterflies land in her hand and visit awhile
It's an Indian Summer and things go up and down daily
The autumnal rainbow is slowly beginning it's spice rack
color show
She likes her iPhone tunes and private fitness time
An October walk in New York
Greeting and playing with every dog or puppy crossing
her path

Different

Always have been and will be
Mostly a loner
It is what I am
Deal with it
Have a Golden Circle of friends
My best friend as a child was my poetry
Other than my husband and BFF
Never lied, hurt, or judged me
Saved my life because all the pain was stored there
All the things I couldn't say were said
I talked to a professional
Saved from depression by my poetry
Still have navy blue days
Along with sleepless nights
His arms are there to rock me and comfort me
My poetry has always been my friend and therapy

Henry's Desk

Taught your books
Believed in your love of Nature and Nurture
Hiked near your beloved pond
As if on cue, the sun came out on that rainy day
Were you saying, Hello, HDT
Then it happened.
I touched your desk
The poetess was in touch with her muse
As you rest near Emerson and the other greats
Just know that touching your desk made me a better
Writer

Valuable Things

Beautiful silence

Unexpected laughter

Unseen rainbows

Cherished friendships both old and new

Mother Nature's and Father Sky's children

Spring weather in the Winter

Magic every moment of the year providing you take the time to notice

No gift wrap

No bows or ribbons

These gifts are valuable things one never will find in a box

His Eyes

How he knew
never know
Heaven sent but when I wasn't looking 39 years ago,
there he was in Whitehead Hall at Brooklyn College
Magic, kismet, whatever you call it
Rainbows, butterflies, stars, and an explosion of joy
We will be married 39 years soon.
Those majestic blue eyes have made me feel like a
princess
even though I still don't see what he sees
Only thing I know is that his eyes still make me lose
control
Deeper part of my soul that makes me almost whole

Goodbye and Farewell *

Life is too short
The cliché is true
Depends on one's interpretation and perspective
Life is too long if you are not living it to the utmost or
living large as they say
Like to think you did
Like to think that you cherished every moment and
enjoyed the zest
Hopefully your dark times found the light to take the
edge off quickly
As we celebrate your departure, though the tears will take
a while to subside
When those rainy days come by we will remember
We won't
remember the goodbyes
We will remember every Hello that was precious and few

In Memory of Ralph Harucki

Dina Marie

She is good to herself and others
Her heart is selfless and courageous
She is a beauty inside and out
Graciousness and kindness define her
She is an incredible soul to share your life with
To be in her presence is a unique experience
One in a million will not describe a number they have
yet to coin
This and so much more is Dina Marie

Genuine Title

Nothing imitation
Completely real
No big deal
Celebrity has no interest
Success is their reward
While others might be bored
Balance is their moniker
Time is enjoyed wisely
Mostly for the greater good
Sometimes greatly misunderstood
In possession of an inner peace and tranquility
Their eyes hold wisdom and knowledge
Quietly persistent
Others fail to accept or see
It's quite sublime
Being genuine

Activate Your Dreams

Years from now you should not have any regrets
Not even a few
Do your thing and participate in life
Speaking as a former spectator
Late bloomer
Call me what you will
Please have many acts
Mistakes show that one is improving
Go for it and even if you fall
You activated your dreams

Takes Your Breath Away

Monarch butterflies landing on flowers
Just the right look coming your way
Swans appearing in unexpected places
Children being real and genuine
Rainbows gracing us with their presence after a storm
An ebony velvet sky with twinkling diamond stars
Rainy day walks that never end
Long summer nights
Moments that stay with us forever
People, places and things beyond compare
The feeling that you've got it right when naysayers tell
you that you're wrong
What captures your heart
Caresses your soul
Knocks you into the next star system

The song you hear on the radio forever
but must stop to sing
Just like you do to me
You always take my breath away

Dedicated to Howie Steinhart

My Happily Ever After

September 14, 1979 was long ago but not to me
Going down a one-way street to a dead end
You lose yourself and your heart
Never coming back again
You never say never because the unexpected
came my way
Might not have fulfilled the requirements of yesterday but
what was made up was more than ever imagined
When you least expect it and stop looking
Prince or Princess Charming appears
The second time around the love of my life and very best
friend
created my happily ever after
My wish is the same for all of you

Acknowledgements

I have been writing poetry since I was eight years old, and while it can be a lonely endeavor, it saved my life. I want to thank my teachers who encouraged me to continue writing poetry, especially James Mangano, my creative writing teacher. I am so grateful for the New York Public Library where I spent many years as a child lost in books and the poetry of Thoreau. I have walked through Walden Pond and touched his desk. He is my muse. I thank Hello Poetry that provides an outlet for poets to get their words out into the world and I am thankful for the individuals who stopped to read mine and left heartfelt comments. I thank my publisher, Cheryl Benton, for her belief in me and her encouragement to create this book. Near and dear to me are my Golden Circle of friends, especially Irene Harucki. And most of all, I thank my husband, soul mate and love of my love, Howard Steinhart, for always being there and supporting me.

About the Poet

Madlyn Epstein Steinhart has been writing poetry since the age of eight. It gave her an internal voice when she felt powerless to speak out. And now she is sharing her voice with others to let them know they are not alone, to encourage them to reach out for help, and to assure them that there is a better tomorrow. Madlyn is a retired New York City public school teacher, a grant writer, and a media literacy specialist. She serves on the board of the National Telemedia Council. *Put Your Boots on and Dance in the Rain* is her debut poetry collection.

The author is donating a portion of the proceeds from the online sales of her book to Bring Change to Mind whose mission is to end the stigma and discrimination surrounding mental illness.

If you enjoy these poems, please leave a review on Amazon.

SELECTED TITLES FROM
THE THREE TOMATOES BOOK PUBLISHING

The Three Tomatoes is an independent publishing company founded to help authors make their books a reality. Visit us at

www.thethreetomatoespublishing.com

With No Regrets: Face It, Live It, Love It by Jane H. Goldman. ISBN: 978-0578548456. This honest, straight from the soul book, will resonate with every woman who's struggled with growing older. In these beautiful and cleverly written essays and poetry, you'll find insights and inspiration for your own journey and living a life without regrets. Available exclusively on Amazon.

Places I Remember: Tales, Truths, Delights from 100 Countries by Lea Lane. ISBN: 978-0578593319. Joyful and informative writings and illustrated photos in a memoir covering over 50 years of travel throughout the world. You'll find a range of unforgettable people and places through vivid personal experiences -- good, bad and often, laugh-out-loud funny. Available on Amazon.

Can You See Us Now? by Cheryl Benton. ISBN: 978-0692054048. Three best friends rebel against unsolicited AARP cards, hot flashes, bosses, becoming invisible, and the perceptions of what's old. Suzy, Trish, and Madge, best friends since their early twenties, seemed to have it all. Beautiful, smart, and successful, they'd made it to the top in the most demanding city of them all, New York. Then they turned 50 and found that the world which once was their oyster started closing up faster than a New York minute. They had suddenly become invisible. Available on Amazon.

Martini Wisdom by Cheryl Benton and Roni Jenkins. ISBN: 978-0578410142. The Martini Ladies are here. Fifty fun and irreverent quips and midlife musings. Martini Wisdom is the perfect anecdote to all those blah, blah, blah motivational and inspirational books about midlife and beyond. It's all those irreverent thought bubbles that the "martini ladies" dare to say out loud. Available on Amazon.

Made in the USA
Monee, IL
09 November 2020

47118360R00080